The Korean War

by Andrew Santella

Content Adviser: Major Peter G. Knight,
Department of History, United States Military Academy,
West Point, New York

Reading Adviser: Rosemary G. Palmer, Ph.D.,
Department of Literacy, College of Education,
Boise State University

COMPASS POINT BOOKS
MINNEAPOLIS, MINNESOTA

Compass Point Books
3109 West 50th Street, #115
Minneapolis, MN 55410

Visit Compass Point Books on the Internet at *www.compasspointbooks.com*
or e-mail your request to *custserv@compasspointbooks.com*

On the cover: With her brother on her back, a weary Korean girl tiredly trudges by a stalled M-26 tank, at Haengju, Korea, on June 9, 1951.

Photographs ©: DVIC/NARA, cover; Prints Old & Rare, back cover (far left); Library of Congress, back cover, 6, 14; The Granger Collection, New York, 5, 18, 32; Hulton-Deutsch Collection/Corbis, 7; Bettmann/Corbis, 10, 13, 25, 27, 29, 36; Howard Sochurek/Time & Life Pictures/Getty Images, 11; Corbis, 17, 24; Hulton Archive/Getty Images, 19, 35; U.S. Marine Corps/Naval Historical Foundation, 21; James Mackey, 22; AFP/Getty Images, 30; Keystone/Getty Images, 33; Central Press/Getty Images, 37; Michael S. Yamashita/Corbis, 39; KCNA via Korean News Service/AFP/Getty Images, 40; Svetlana Zhurkin, 41.

Editor: Julie Gassman
Page Production: Noumenon Creative
Photo Researcher: Svetlana Zhurkin
Cartographer: XNR Productions, Inc.
Library Consultant: Kathleen Baxter

Creative Director: Keith Griffin
Editorial Director: Carol Jones
Managing Editor: Catherine Neitge

Library of Congress Cataloging-in-Publication Data
Santella, Andrew.
  The Korean War/ by Andrew Santella
     p. cm.—(We the people)
  Includes bibliographical references and index.
  ISBN-13: 978-0-7565-2027-4 (hardcover)
  ISBN-10: 0-7565-2027-4 (hardcover)
  ISBN-13: 978-0-7565-2039-7 (paperback)
  ISBN-10: 0-7565-2039-8 (paperback)
  1. Korean War, 1950–1953—Juvenile literature. I. Title. II. We the People (Series)
(Compass Point Books)
  DS918.S25 2007
  951.904'2—dc22   2006006767

TABLE OF CONTENTS

THE WORLD SURPRISED

It was another Sunday in the middle of Korea's rainy season. In the dark hours before dawn on June 25, 1950, a steady rain fell along the border between North Korea and South Korea. Now and then, the sound of gunfire broke the quiet. But this alone was no reason for alarm. For months, North Korean and South Korean troops had been fighting in small border skirmishes. Short bursts of gunfire seemed almost as common as the rain.

But this time, the gunfire did not stop. Instead, the fighting spread to other points along the border. Heavy artillery joined in the battle. Then about 90,000 North Korean troops crossed the border into South Korea and began streaming to the south. This was no ordinary border clash. This was an invasion. North Korea had launched a massive attack on its neighbor to the south.

As more North Korean troops poured over the border, others attacked South Korea by sea. Within hours, North Korea had seized the South Korean city of Kaesong. By noon, South Korea's capital city, Seoul, was under attack.

A 1950 editorial cartoon predicted the explosive result of war following the North Korean invasion of South Korea on June 25.

President Harry S. Truman

South Korea's military was caught completely unprepared. So was the country's most powerful ally, the United States. U.S. President Harry S. Truman later recalled how the invasion had shocked him. "It was a complete surprise to me, as it was to nearly everybody else even all over the world. Nobody thought any such thing would take place."

Now President Truman and other U.S. leaders faced the difficult decision of how to respond to the invasion. Should the United States rush to help defend South Korea? And if the U.S. military did join the fight, would it be able to stop the North Korean advance? In the first hours of the Korean War, there were no easy answers.

A NATION DIVIDED

North Korea and South Korea had not always been divided. In fact, the Korean peninsula had been united as a single country for centuries. Koreans called their country Choson, which means "the land of the morning calm." The country was rarely calm, however. For centuries, Korea was unable to fight off stronger countries seeking to expand their empires. China and Japan took turns invading and dominating the peninsula country. For both,

Thatched roofs covered buildings in a typical Korean town in 1910.

7

Korea served as an invasion route toward the other. Finally in 1910, Japan took control of Korea and made it part of its growing empire.

When Japan was defeated in World War II (1939–1945), its empire fell. The United States and the Soviet Union took control of lands that the Japanese had ruled. Korea was split in two. Soviet troops occupied the northern half of Korea, while U.S. troops occupied the southern half. To divide the two sections of Korea roughly in half, a U.S. official picked out a line on a map to serve as a boundary. He chose a line called the 38th parallel.

In the years after World War II, the Soviet Union and the United States were engaged in a conflict called the Cold War. The United States and its allies favored open, democratic government. The Soviet Union and its allies practiced a system of government called communism. Both the Soviets and the Americans tried to expand their power around the globe. But their rivalry did not erupt into actual fighting. Instead, the Cold War was largely a battle of words and ideas between the United States and the Soviet Union. The Soviets gave military support to other countries that set up communist governments. At the same

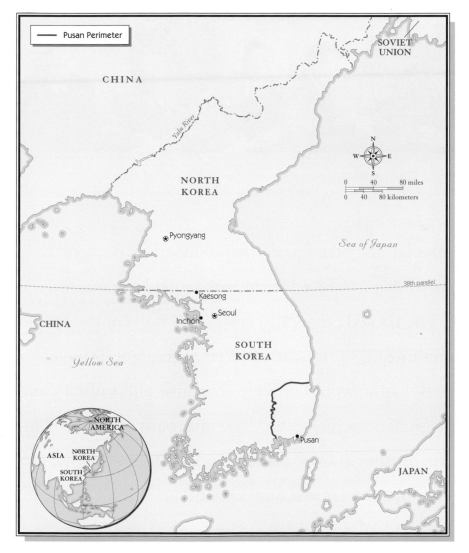

The Korean peninsula sits between China and Japan.

President Truman asked Congress for $400 million to defend the countries of Greece and Turkey from communist pressure. This request grew into the Truman Doctrine.

time, the United States and other democratic powers supported democratic governments around the world.

The United States also worked to prevent the spread of communist governments. In 1947, President Truman declared that he would provide economic and military aid to foreign nations threatened by communist takeover. This promise became known as the Truman Doctrine. It was in Korea that the United States would act on this doctrine and the Cold War would erupt into open conflict.

THE PATH TO WAR

The line dividing North Korea and South Korea was supposed to be temporary. Members of various Korean political parties discussed their visions for a unified Korea. However, they disagreed about the direction their country should take. Korean political leaders turned to either the United States or the Soviet Union for support. As a result, North Korea and South Korea followed different paths.

North Korean leader, Kim Il Sung (bottom, far right), was supported with a group of Soviet military advisers.

In North Korea, the Soviet occupiers made Kim Il Sung the premier and created a Soviet-style communist government called the Democratic People's Republic of Korea. To support it, they created a huge North Korean army. The Soviet Union supported the army, known as the North Korean People's Army (NKPA), by equipping it with Russian tanks and artillery.

In South Korea, national elections were held in 1948. The elections established the new Republic of Korea and made Syngman Rhee the country's first president. The United States supported the new Republic of Korea, but it did not offer the kind of military help that the Soviets offered to North Korea. The South Korean army could not match North Korea's in tanks or aircraft.

Korea remained split in two. From across the border, the governments of North Korea and South Korea viewed each other with suspicion and distrust. Some observers in other countries feared that civil war would break out in Korea. But U.S. military leaders did

South Koreans waited in long lines to vote in the nation's first election.

not believe that North Korea would invade South Korea.
In fact, the United States had removed all but about 500
troops from South Korea.

In 1949, North Korean leader Kim Il Sung secretly received permission from communist leaders in the Soviet Union and China to invade South Korea. The invasion

Kim Il Sung asked communist leaders for permission to invade South Korea during a 1949 visit to the Soviet Union.

14

began the following year. When it came, South Korea proved unready to defend itself. Of South Korea's 95,000 troops, about one-third were away from their posts on leave. The roughly 63,000 soldiers who remained were not enough to stop the NKPA invasion force of 90,000. The South Korean defense quickly crumbled.

President Truman was spending the weekend relaxing with his family at his home in Independence, Missouri, when he learned of the invasion. He rushed back to Washington, D.C., and met with his advisers to discuss the U.S. response. Some military aides advised him not to get involved in the war. Korea was halfway around the world and of little strategic value, they told him.

But Truman worried that if the United States did nothing to stop the invasion, communist powers would try to invade other countries. He wanted to show America's allies that the United States would defend democratic nations from outside interference. Truman vowed to turn back the invasion.

THE UNITED NATIONS

President Truman turned to the United Nations for help. On June 25, 1950—the same day as the invasion—the United States introduced a resolution in the United Nations Security Council. It urged members of this international peacekeeping organization to support driving the North Koreans out of South Korea. The Security Council voted 9-0 to help South Korea. That same day, Truman announced that the U.S. Air Force and Navy would support South Korea's military. He did not send troops to fight on the ground, however, because the use of ground troops was more likely to result in heavy American casualties.

The invasion continued. North Korean troops captured Seoul, South Korea's capital city. Soon nearly all of South Korea would belong to North Korea. On June 30, Truman decided to send U.S. ground troops to join the fight. He acted without asking Congress to declare war.

U.N. Security Council members raised their hands in support of the resolution to drive North Korea out of South Korea.

The U.S. Constitution gives Congress—not the president—the power to make declarations of war. But in this case, Truman used his authority as commander in chief of the military to send the troops, without ever speaking of war. In fact, even though American troops would fight and

The June 28, 1950, issue of The New York Times *reported the U.S. involvement in Korea.*

die in Korea for three years, Congress never made a formal declaration of war.

On July 7, the United Nations called on its members to help turn back the North Koreans. Twenty nations responded by sending combat units, medical teams, and other help to South Korea. Soldiers from all the countries would fight as part of a joint command, which was led by the United States. Truman named General Douglas MacArthur to com-mand all the U.N. forces in South Korea. MacArthur, who had proven himself

General Douglas MacArthur

during World War I and World War II, held the highest rank given by the U.S. Army as a five-star general.

Even with the aid of other countries, the fight to help South Korea was mostly an American effort. Most of the air power, naval power, and ground forces came from the United States. But enlisting the support of the United Nations and its member nations was important. It showed that much of the world was unified in resisting the North Korean invasion.

In the first days of the war, it seemed that nothing could stop the North Koreans. The first American troops rushed into combat in Korea were inexperienced and lacked proper training. They suffered many defeats and had to retreat again and again. By early August, the North Koreans had pushed the defenders to the southeastern tip of the Korean peninsula. There the troops organized a desperate defense. They knew that retreating further would leave all of Korea in North Korea's possession.

"There will be no more retreating," U.S. General Walton Walker said. Now the U.N. defenders set up a 150-mile-long (240-kilometer) defensive line called the Pusan Perimeter. Their hope was to defend that line until more troops could arrive to reinforce them. Wherever the North Koreans attacked along the line, the U.N. defenders

Two American soldiers observed operations during the defense of the Pusan Perimeter.

rushed to meet them and push them back.

Finally, help began to arrive. Troops from Great
Britain joined the fight on the U.N. side. For the first time
in the war, the defenders were able to field an army as
large as North Korea's. U.S. air forces took control of the
skies over Korea. The success along the Pusan Perimeter
gave the U.N. forces hope for the first time.

LANDING AT INCHON

General MacArthur came up with a bold plan to build on the Pusan Perimeter success. He would launch a counterattack deep behind North Korean lines. U.N. troops would travel by sea to the port city of Inchon. Although far behind the battle lines, Inchon was just 20 miles (32 km) west of Seoul. From there they could storm the beaches and begin moving inland to recapture Seoul.

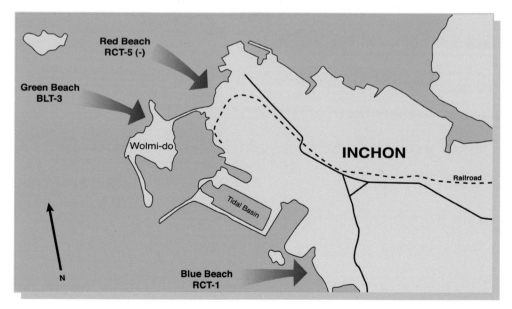

A map shows the invasion routes for the landing at Inchon.

It was a dangerous gamble. The port had several physical challenges, including a narrow entry point and violent currents, that made landing there difficult. Even some of MacArthur's generals thought the plan was a bad idea. If any part of the plan went wrong, the U.N. troops could easily be wiped out. But MacArthur insisted the plan would work. "We shall land at Inchon, and I shall crush them," he promised.

On September 13, U.S. and British destroyer ships began firing on North Korean positions near Inchon. The attack was so intense that it left many North Korean defenders ready to surrender.

Then early on September 15, hundreds of U.S. and British ships began carrying more than 70,000 U.S. Marines and other U.N. troops toward the shore at Inchon. Landing crafts carried the Marines to the beaches, and from there they rushed ashore. Some troops used ladders to scale the high concrete walls that protected parts of Inchon from the sea. Some attacked North Korean machine gun

U.S. and British ships sped toward the beaches of Inchon.

nests. In some cases, they found the North Koreans waiting with their arms raised in surrender.

MacArthur's plan worked perfectly. As the Marines moved ashore, ships carried tanks, bulldozers, and other equipment to the beaches to support them. North Koreans put up a weak resistance. Within hours, the U.N. forces had taken Inchon, captured hundreds of prisoners, and suffered light casualties. Within two weeks, they had pushed the North Koreans out of Seoul and sent them into full retreat. By October, the North Koreans had been driven back across the 38th parallel. MacArthur's risky plan had turned the tide of the war. Finally, the North Koreans were on the defensive.

This success left the U.N. forces with a difficult decision: Should they pursue the NKPA north past the 38th parallel and into North Korea? Or was their mission

Debris filled the streets of Seoul in early October 1950.

complete now that the North Koreans had been driven out of South Korea? South Korean president Syngman Rhee wanted the U.N. forces to keep fighting and to create "one Korea." Truman agreed, and the U.N. Security Council supported this decision in a resolution passed on October 7. U.N. forces invaded North Korea and captured more territory. On October 19, they took North Korea's capital, Pyongyang.

These new developments worried China's leader, Mao Tse-tung. As the head of a communist power, he did not like seeing U.N. troops rolling through North Korea. He feared they might even attack China itself. Mao ordered Chinese troops to mass along the Yalu River, which forms the border between China and North Korea.

Late in October, the Chinese army, known as the Chinese Communist Forces (CCF), began moving over the border into North Korea. The Chinese battled American and U.N. troops for the first time on October 25. The Chinese scored a victory, paused, and faded back into the mountains of North Korea as quickly as they had emerged. MacArthur was reassured by the retreat. With Truman's full approval, he launched another attack. But the CCF fought back in overwhelming numbers. The Americans and other U.N. forces found themselves retreating again. "We face an entirely new war," General MacArthur said.

More than 10,000 Seoul citizens gathered to protest the Chinese involvement in the Korean War.

27

THE NEW WAR

American and U.N. troops faced a terrible challenge. The Chinese fielded a huge army of 300,000 soldiers. They fought fiercely and attacked in waves that never seemed to let up—no matter how many casualties they suffered. As they advanced, they often blew whistles and bugles to signal to each other. U.N. troops came to dread the noise that went along with the deadly Chinese attacks.

The U.N. forces also had to deal with a brutal Korean winter. Bitterly cold weather made it difficult to march, sleep, or even eat. One Marine sergeant later remembered how bare hands would freeze onto the steel weapons. Others recalled snow and ice freezing on their faces as they marched, sometimes even freezing their mouths shut. U.S. troops fought bravely as they retreated south.

As the retreat continued, thousands of Korean refugees followed behind the troops. These ordinary Koreans were trying to avoid the destruction and danger

U.S. Marines endured Korea's subzero winter temperatures.

of the war. But Communist forces sometimes dressed like civilians to blend into the population to both avoid and carry out attacks. Before this war, American troops had never faced such guerrilla tactics. It was often difficult for soldiers to tell if they were encountering the enemy or innocent civilians.

Korean refugees fled past frozen rice fields in their journey south.

By January 1951, the Chinese had recaptured all of
North Korea and part of South Korea, including Seoul.
The U.N. forces fought back, and both sides suffered
terrible casualties. Meanwhile, American leaders began to
disagree about the conduct of the war. General MacArthur

thought it was time to take the war to China. He wanted permission to bomb the communist country. But President Truman believed that the war should be fought only in Korea. "We are trying to prevent a third world war," he said. The president feared attacking China could mark the start of World War III.

MacArthur openly disagreed with the president. He feared that Truman would let the war end with the two sides right back where they were when the conflict started. MacArthur wanted a clear-cut victory. He believed that his troops had fought and died for nothing less. He even did his best to break up Truman's efforts at peace talks. In March, MacArthur publicly threatened the Chinese with a full-scale war. He also questioned the ability of the Chinese army to defend China.

While MacArthur was speaking out against China, Truman was trying to arrange peace talks with the communist country. But MacArthur's tough talk angered the Chinese and hurt the opportunity for peace talks. His statements also undermined the president's authority.

Finally, Truman had enough. On April 11, the president announced that he had relieved MacArthur of his command "so that there would be no doubt or confusion as to the real purpose and aim of our policy." Truman knew that the U.S. military had to accept his leadership and

The New York Times *reported the news of MacArthur's dismissal.*

follow only his plan.

Truman was widely criticized for his decision to fire the general. MacArthur returned to the United States and received a hero's welcome from cheering crowds. Truman responded that "the cause of world peace is more important than any individual."

General Matthew Ridgway

Command of U.N. troops fell to General Matthew Ridgway. Ridgway was a capable leader. A month earlier he had led a group of U.N. troops in recapturing Seoul. This was the fourth and final time the city changed hands during the war.

PEACE TALKS

By summer 1951, Korea was a landscape of barbed wire and trenches. Both the countryside and the cities were badly damaged by bombardments. Finally, the two sides agreed to begin truce talks on July 10. But both sides remained distrustful, and little progress was made toward peace. Meanwhile, the fighting and killing continued on the front lines.

The main conflict in the peace talks was over the return of prisoners of war. The communist nations insisted that all Chinese and North Korean soldiers who had been captured by the United Nations must be returned when the fighting ended. But the United States argued that many Chinese and North Korean soldiers did not want to return to their home countries.

U.S. leaders claimed that these soldiers did not want to go back to countries where they would not have political freedom. "We will not buy an armistice by turning over

human beings for slaughter and slavery," Truman said.
The war continued for another 18 months. During that
time, 9,000 U.S. soldiers lost their lives.

In April 1953, the two sides agreed to exchange
sick and wounded prisoners. Not long after this, they
agreed that no prisoner of war would be forced to return
to his home country against his will. Any prisoner who

North Korean prisoners of war made baskets in a South Korean prison.

American troops celebrated after hearing news of the cease-fire.

did not want to return home would be granted asylum in another country.

A cease-fire was declared to end the fighting on July 27, 1953. More than three years had passed since the war started. Much of the Korean peninsula was left in ruins. Thousands of Koreans were left homeless. More than

1 million South Korean and an unknown number of North Korean civilians died as a result of the war. U.S. military personnel losses were high, with more than 33,665 soldiers dying.

U.N. forces eventually returned 75,823 prisoners to China and North Korea. The communist forces returned 12,773 American, South Korean, and U. N. prisoners.

The United Nations and communist forces exchanged groups of prisoners on August 11, 1953, in Panmunjom, Korea.

More than 21,000 prisoners from the communist countries chose not to return home, while only 347 U.N. prisoners elected not to return home.

Korea remained divided. In fact, at war's end, each side controlled almost the same territory it held at the start of the war. South Korea ended up gaining a small area of about 1,500 square miles (3,900 square km).

Korea is still divided today. A heavily fortified border runs between the two countries near the 38th parallel. A 2½-mile-wide (4-km) demilitarized zone (DMZ) extends all along the border. Military forces and operations are banned from this area, which is designed to keep the armies of the two nations apart.

North and South Korea have followed very different paths in the years since the war. South Korea is a stable democracy with a strong economy. It remains an ally of the United States.

In contrast, North Korea has suffered under the dictatorships of Kim Il Sung and his son Kim Jong Il.

Small rocks are placed on the fence of the demilitarized zone that separates North and South Korea. The rocks serve as an indication of passage attempts.

In the late 1990s, 2.5 million North Koreans died from famine. The country has continued to suffer severe food shortages, and many of its poorest people enjoy little political freedom or hope for improvement.

Despite these problems, North Korea has one of the largest militaries in the world, with more than 1 million

North Korean leader Kim Jong Il

soldiers in the army. Also, North Korea's leaders are working to develop nuclear weapons— among the most powerful and deadly weapons in the world. This alarms leaders in the United States and other countries. They don't trust North Korea's leaders with the power that goes along with such weapons.

The Korean War is sometimes called the Forgotten War. It is often overshadowed in history books by World War II, the bloodiest war in history, and the Vietnam War, a controversial conflict that the United States lost. To honor the sacrifices of Americans who fought in the

Korean War, the National Park Service opened the Korean War Veterans Memorial in Washington, D.C., in 1995. Millions of people visit the memorial each year. By educating visitors about the war, the memorial helps ensure that the Korean War will no longer be a forgotten war.

The Korean War Memorial includes life-size statues of 19 ground soldiers, ready for battle.

41

GLOSSARY

artillery—large guns, such as cannons, that require several soldiers to load, aim, and fire

asylum—protection given to refugees from another country

casualties—soldiers killed, captured, or injured during a war

civilians—people not part of a military force

communism—a system in which goods and property are owned by the government and shared in common

controversial—causing dispute or disagreement

guerrilla tactics—warfare using small, surprise attacks rather than large battles

landing crafts—boats used to bring troops ashore from larger ships

parallel—an imaginary numbered circle on Earth's surface that marks the distance north or south of the equator

skirmishes—small battles

DID YOU KNOW?

- The Korean War marked the first use of Mobile Army Surgical Hospitals, or MASH units. In MASH units, soldiers wounded in the war were given medical care very close to the front lines.

- The war became an issue in the 1952 presidential race between Republican Dwight D. Eisenhower and Democrat Adlai Stevenson. Eisenhower vowed to travel to Korea personally to look for a way to end the war. He was elected president in November 1952 and went to Korea to meet with American troops for three days the following year.

- The Korean War Veterans Memorial in Washington, D.C., depicts 19 members of U.S. armed forces on patrol in Korea. The inscription reads: "Our nation honors her sons and daughters who answered the call to defend a country they never knew and a people they never met."

- The Korean Demilitarized Zone (DMZ) contains approximately 1 million land mines, highly explosive devices buried just underground. It is one of the most heavily mined areas on Earth.

IMPORTANT DATES

Timeline

1945	Korea is split into U.S. and Soviet zones.
1948	On August 12, the Republic of Korea (South Korea) is formed; on September 9, the Democratic People's Republic of Korea (North Korea) is formed.
1950	On June 25, North Korea invades South Korea; on June 30, President Harry S. Truman orders U.S. ground forces to defend South Korea; on September 15, U.N. troops capture Inchon; on October 14, Chinese troops enter North Korea.
1951	In January, communist forces recapture Seoul; on March 18, U.N. troops retake Seoul; in July, peace talks begin.
1952	Peace talks stop because of disagreements over prisoners of war.
1953	Cease-fire agreement brings an end to Korean War.

IMPORTANT PEOPLE

KIM IL SUNG (1912–1994)

First premier of the Democratic People's Republic of Korea (North Korea); as a dictator, he tightly controlled many parts of North Korean society

DOUGLAS MACARTHUR (1880–1964)

General who commanded U.N. forces in Korea until President Truman removed him from command; he led troops in the landing at Inchon, which helped turn the tide of the war

MAO TSE-TUNG (1893–1976)

Founder of the People's Republic of China who sent Chinese troops to Korea in support of the North Korean People's Army

SYNGMAN RHEE (1875–1965)

First president of the Republic of Korea (South Korea); as an anti-communist, he had a strong desire to unite Korea as a democracy

HARRY S. TRUMAN (1884–1972)

Thirty-third president of the United States; he involved U.S. troops in the Korean War and asked members of the United Nations for support

WANT TO KNOW MORE?

At the Library

Ashabranner, Brent K. *Remembering Korea: The Korean War Veterans Memorial.* Brookfield, Conn.: Twenty-First Century Books, 2001.

Cannarella, Deborah. *Harry S. Truman.* Minneapolis: Compass Point Books, 2003.

Feldman, Ruth Tenzer. *The Korean War.* Minneapolis: Lerner Publications Co., 2004.

Stein, R. Conrad. *The Korean War Veterans Memorial.* New York: Children's Press, 2002.

On the Web

For more information on *The Korean War*, use FactHound to track down Web sites related to this book.

1. Go to *www.facthound.com*

2. Type in a search word related to this book or this book ID: 0756520274

3. Click on the *Fetch It* button.

Your trusty FactHound will fetch the best Web sites for you!

On the Road

Korean War Veterans National Museum & Library
1007 Pacesetter Drive
Rantoul, IL 61866
888/295-7212
Books, manuscripts, maps, photographs, and military and civilian documents associated with the Korean War

The Korean War Veterans Memorial
900 Ohio Drive SW
Washington, DC 20024
202/426-6841
National memorial dedicated to the soldiers who fought in the Korean War

Look for more We the People books about this era:

The 19th Amendment
ISBN 0-7565-1260-3

The Berlin Airlift
ISBN 0-7565-2024-X

The Dust Bowl
ISBN 0-7565-0837-1

Ellis Island
ISBN 0-7565-0302-7

The Great Depression
ISBN 0-7565-0152-0

Navajo Code Talkers
ISBN 0-7565-0611-5

Pearl Harbor
ISBN 0-7565-0680-8

The Persian Gulf War
ISBN 0-7565-0612-3

September 11
ISBN 0-7565-2029-0

The Sinking of the USS Indianapolis
ISBN 0-7565-2031-2

The Statue of Liberty
ISBN 0-7565-0100-8

The Titanic
ISBN 0-7565-0614-X

The Tuskegee Airmen
ISBN 0-7565-0683-2

Vietnam Veterans Memorial
ISBN 0-7565-2032-0

A complete list of We the People titles is available on our Web site:
www.compasspointbooks.com

INDEX

About the Author

Andrew Santella writes for magazines and newspapers, including *GQ* and the *New York Times Book Review*. He is the author of a number of books for young readers. He lives outside Chicago with his wife and son.